D1202066

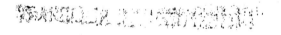

HISTORY IN LITERATURE

THE STORY BEHIND...

HARPER LEE'S
TO KILL A
MOCKINGBIRD

Bryon Giddens-White

Heinemann Library
Chicago, Illinois

(handwritten) 813 GID GIDDENS-WHITE HARPER LEE'S TO KILL A MOCKINGBIRD 10-22-07 C.1 HEINEMANN $23.00

Customer Service 888–454–2279

Visit our website at www.heinemannlibrary.com

Designed by Richard Parker and Tinstar Design
Printed in China by Leo Paper Group

11 10 09 08 07
10 9 8 7 6 5 4 3 2 1

Library of Congress Cataloging-in-Publication Data
Giddens-White, Bryon.
  The story behind Harper Lee's To kill a mockingbird / Bryon Giddens-White.
     p. cm. -- (History in literature)
  Includes bibliographical references and index.
  ISBN 1-4034-8208-X (lib. bdg.)
  1. Lee, Harper. To kill a mockingbird--Juvenile literature. 2. Lee, Harper--Juvenile literature. 3. United States--Race relations--History--Juvenile literature. I. Title. II. Series.

  PS3562.E353T63345 2006
  813'.54--dc22

                        2006004669

Acknowledgments
The publishers would like to thank the following for permission to reproduce photographs/ quotes: Advertising Archive p. 5; Bridgeman Art Library p. 36 (White House, Washington D.C., USA), p. 39 (Museo di Goethe, Rome, Italy, Giraudon); Corbis pp. 14, 17, 19, 31; Corbis pp. 8, 12, 16, 18, 20, 21, 22, 24, 25, 26, 27, 28, 32, 35, 38, 42, 44 (Bettman); Corbis p. 9 (Underwood & Underwood), 43 (George McCarthy), 49 (Katy Winn), 45 (Rick Friedman); Corbis Sygma p. 46 (R. Jaap/Beaumont Enterprise); Getty Images pp. 30 (Charles Hewitt), 11, 33 (Hulton Archive), 37 (Hulton Archive/R. Gates), 15 (MPI), 23 (Time Life Pictures/Carl Iwasaki), 6, 10 (Time Life Pictures/Donald Uhrbrock), 7 (Time Life Pictures/Lisa Larson); Mitchell Jamieson, An Incident in Contemporary American Life, 1942 U.S. Department of the Interior Museum, Washington, D.C., David Allison, photographer p. 29; The Kobal Collection pp. 40, 41 (Universal), 48 (UA/Infinity/Baron/Dory, Attila).

Cover photograph of Harper Lee reproduced with permission of Getty Images/Hulton Archive. Background photos reproduced with permission of Photos.com; istockphoto.com/Marje Cannon.

The publishers would like to thank Dr Claudia Durst Johnson for her assistance in the preparation of this book.

Every effort has been made to contact copyright holders of any material reproduced in this book. Any omissions will be rectified in subsequent printings if notice is given to the publisher.

Disclaimer
All the Internet addresses (URLs) given in this book were valid at the time of going to press. However, due to the dynamic nature of the Internet, some addresses may have changed or ceased to exist since publication. While the author and publishers regret any inconvenience this may cause readers, no responsibility for any such changes can be accepted by either the author or the publishers.

Contents

Some words are shown in bold, **like this**. You can find out what they mean by looking in the glossary.

The Life of an Author and Her Novel

During the 1950s, Harper Lee began work on a series of short stories. The stories took place in a small southern American town during the **Great Depression**. Lee, in her twenties at the time, based the stories on her childhood experiences in Alabama. By the end of the 1950s, she had worked the stories into a novel, called *To Kill a Mockingbird*, which was published in the summer of 1960.

The novel's narrator is a woman named Jean Louise Finch. Jean Louise, nicknamed "Scout," relates scenes and events that happened during three years of her childhood. She explains them as she experienced them at the time—that is, through the eyes of a child.

The **narrative** features two interwoven stories. One is about Scout, her brother, Jem, and their friend Dill's growing fascination with a neighborhood **recluse** named Arthur "Boo" Radley. The other story is about an African-American man named Tom Robinson. A poor white girl named Mayella Ewell falsely accuses Robinson of rape. Scout's widowed father, Atticus, is the brave lawyer appointed to defend Robinson in court.

Both stories are related to Lee's own life and to the historical circumstances in which she wrote. Lee grew up in Monroeville, a small Alabama town very much like the fictional town of Maycomb. Lee's father, like Scout's, was a lawyer and a representative in the Alabama state legislature.

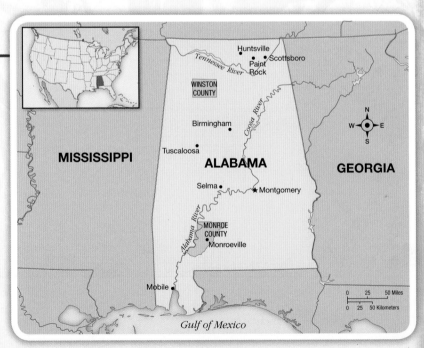

Harper Lee grew up in the United States' Deep South, in the town of Monroeville. Monroeville is a small town in southwest Alabama, about halfway between the major cities of Montgomery and Mobile.

The first edition of *To Kill a Mockingbird*, published by J. B. Lippincott, featured a dust jacket designed by Shirley Smith. A picture of Harper Lee taken by the writer Truman Capote appeared on the back. This is the cover of a 1960s edition.

Racial injustice

The trial of Tom Robinson has parallels with other trials that occurred in Alabama during Lee's childhood. In the infamous Scottsboro case (see page 22) of the 1930s, two white women accused nine African-American youths of rape. Medical examiners found no evidence that a rape had occurred, and one of the women later admitted that she had lied. Nevertheless, even the luckiest of the accused spent six years in prison before going free.

To Kill a Mockingbird

Harper Lee

Pulitzer Prize winner as 1960's best novel. 82 weeks in U.S.A. best-seller list. Over 5,000,000 (five million) copies sold! There's been nothing like this book since 'Gone with the Wind'

Such injustice was still common during Lee's adulthood. In 1955, a young African-American boy from Chicago named Emmett Till was brutally murdered while visiting relatives in Mississippi (see pages 24–25). Till's offence was whistling at a white woman. An all-white jury quickly set Till's murderers free.

The murder of Emmett Till was a **catalyst** for the U.S. **civil rights movement**. This movement aimed to achieve racial equality and to end **segregation** in the South.

The civil rights movement was heating up during the period in which Lee wrote *To Kill a Mockingbird*. This may be one reason why the novel found such an interested audience. In its first year, *To Kill a Mockingbird* sold half a million copies. In 1961, it won the prestigious **Pulitzer Prize** for literature and, a year later, Universal Studios made the novel into an enormously popular film.

Tay Hohoff was an **editor** who worked with Lee on *To Kill a Mockingbird*. Hohoff said that Lee considered her novel "a love story pure and simple." She then added that:

[The novel] is written out of [Lee's] love for the South, but it is also the story of a father's love for his children, and the love they gave in return, full measure and running over. There are more meanings to the word 'love' than the romantic one, and it is to these other meanings that Harper Lee has chosen to address herself in **To Kill a Mockingbird**.

Other themes

Lee's novel explores other themes besides race and justice. These include childhood, education, family, religion, and what it means to be a woman. *To Kill a Mockingbird*'s themes and stories are rooted in Lee's personal experiences and in the historical era in which she lived and worked.

The Lees and the Finches

Nelle Harper Lee was born in Monroeville, Alabama, on April 28, 1926. About 1,000 people lived in Monroeville when Lee was born. Today, the town has a population of about 7,000.

Lee was the youngest of four children. She had two sisters and one brother. Their mother was Frances Finch Lee. Lee used the name Finch for Atticus's family in *To Kill a Mockingbird*. Little is known about Lee's mother, though she is said to have had a fondness for playing piano and doing crossword puzzles. Lee's sister Alice, however, has said that their mother suffered from a serious "nervous disorder."

More is known about Lee's father, Amasa Coleman Lee. Lee used her father as the model for the character of Atticus Finch. Like Atticus, Lee's father was well into his forties when his youngest daughter was born. Many who knew him say that Amasa Lee had qualities like those of the novel's hero. He is remembered as a man of great dignity who was warm-hearted and humble, and a good citizen.

Amasa Coleman Lee (1880–1962)

Lee's father, Amasa Coleman Lee, was born on July 19, 1880, in Butler County, Alabama. He moved to Monroeville in the early 1900s and started practicing law in 1915. From 1927 until 1939, he served in the Alabama state legislature. He also managed to find time to edit the **Monroe Journal** *from 1929 until 1947. A. C. Lee died on April 15, 1962, at the age of 81. In the dedication of* **To Kill a Mockingbird** *Harper Lee wrote "for Mr. Lee and Alice, in consideration of Love & Affection." In this photo, Lee relaxes with his daughter not long after the novel's publication.*

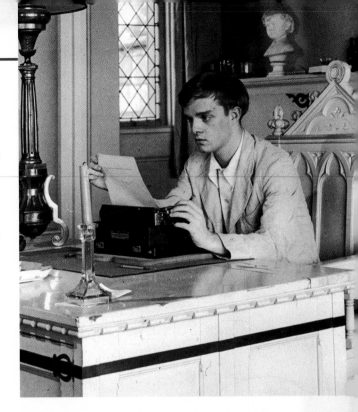

Lee acknowledged that her childhood friend Truman Capote was the model for Dill in *To Kill a Mockingbird.* Capote was also a writer. He is seen here in 1946 working on his first novel *Other Voices, Other Rooms.* In 1959, while Lee awaited the publication of her novel, she began to help Capote conduct interviews that he later used to write his best-known work: *In Cold Blood.*

Many of Lee's characters are said to be based upon real people. Young Nelle, for example, is said to have been a **tomboy**, like the narrator Scout. Also like Scout, Lee was a child of the Great Depression. As a young girl, Lee also befriended a boy—Truman Capote—who lived next door with his aunts. However, people who know Lee say she is upset by these comparisons.

Exchanging law for literature

After graduating from high school, Lee spent a year at Huntingdon College in Montgomery. In 1945, she transferred to the University of Alabama at Tuscaloosa. Two years later, she entered the university's law school. In 1949, however, just six months away from earning her degree, Lee decided to quit school and pursue a writing career.

Soon after leaving law school, Lee moved to New York City, where she took a job as an airline reservations clerk. For several years, she worked during the day and spent her evenings writing.

In 1963, Lee told one interviewer:

> *The minute [...] I started to study law, I loathed it. I always wanted to be a writer.*

A Christmas present

In 1956, close friends offered to support Lee financially for a year. Their help allowed Lee to begin writing and refining her stories about small-town life in the South. Within a year, Lee produced the first draft of a novel, and sent the draft to the publisher J. B. Lippincott. The publisher took an interest and invited Lee for a meeting.

Lippincott's editors told Lee that they were impressed with her writing. However, they felt that her **manuscript** seemed more like a collection of short stories than a proper novel. Lee agreed to revise her work, and, after many revisions, Lippincott offered Lee a contract. She then spent another two and a half years polishing and perfecting what would become *To Kill a Mockingbird*.

Scout's 1930s childhood

Lee's novel opens in the summer of 1933 and ends in October 1935. Lee does not reveal the exact dates right away, but she does provide clues that allow readers to guess that the novel is set during the Great Depression.

The first clue is the mention of "Hoover carts"—old cars that were pulled by mules because their owners couldn't afford fuel. After mentioning Hoover carts, Scout offers a second clue when she reports that, "Maycomb County had recently been told that it had nothing to fear but fear itself." These remarks come from a speech given by President Hoover's successor, Franklin Delano Roosevelt. Roosevelt became president in March 1933.

Many Americans believed that President Herbert Hoover did little to help them during the Great Depression. During his presidency from 1929 to 1933, Hoover's name became associated with poverty. Shantytowns (poor areas of a city made up mostly of huts), which sprang up to shelter the homeless, were called "Hoovervilles." "Hoover blankets" were newspapers under which the poor slept. This photo shows a Hooverville in Seattle, 1934.

During his inaugural address on March 4, 1933 (left), Roosevelt offered words of encouragement to the U.S. people: "This great nation will endure as it has endured, will revive and will prosper. So, first of all, let me assert my firm belief that the only thing we have to fear is fear itself." The U.S. people needed encouragement. They were suffering through what would become the longest and most severe economic crisis ever experienced by the Western world—the Great Depression.

Two interwoven stories

After establishing the setting, Lee gives a history of the Finches. Maycomb's Finches include Atticus and his children—Jem and Jean Louise. They treat their African-American housekeeper, Calpurnia, like a member of the family as well. Jem is ten when the novel begins. Scout is about four years younger.

Because Scout is so young, she doesn't always understand what is going on around her. But her questions and observations are sharp enough to allow readers to understand what is happening by "reading between the lines."

Readers learn that Arthur "Boo" Radley broke the law when he was a teenager. When his father, Nathan Radley, heard about it, he kept Boo at home and would not let him go out. Legend has it that fifteen years later, Boo stabbed his father in the leg with a pair of scissors. After that, Boo spent time locked in Maycomb's courthouse basement before vanishing once more into the Radley home. The children are fascinated by the myth and mystery of Boo.

The story of Tom Robinson first begins to unfold in the schoolyard. Though she hardly understands what is happening, Scout fights other students who insult her father for agreeing to defend Robinson in the rape trial.

Harper Lee may have had the rooms of Monroeville's old courthouse in mind as she wrote about the trial of Tom Robinson. When Universal Studios made Lee's novel into a movie, they built a replica of Monroeville's courtroom in which to film the trial.

Racism in the courts

We learn more after Scout, Jem, and Dill sneak into the courtroom to watch the trial. **Testimony** reveals that it was actually Mayella Ewell who had a love interest in Robinson. This interest broke a strong **taboo** that made contact between African-American men and white women almost unthinkable. When Bob Ewell discovers his daughter trying to seduce Robinson, he is outraged and forces her to accuse Tom Robinson of rape.

In spite of Atticus's skillful defense, an all-white jury convicts Robinson. Atticus asks Robinson to stay hopeful. He is planning an appeal, which he thinks has a good chance of success. But Robinson tries to escape from prison. Prison guards shoot Robinson seventeen times, killing him.

Robinson's conviction and death do not satisfy Bob Ewell. He feels humiliated by the trial and wants revenge. Finally, he attacks Jem and Scout as they return home from a Halloween pageant. Boo Radley sees the attack and leaves his home to protect the children. In the process of defending Jem and Scout, Boo kills Ewell.

In the stories and events surrounding Robinson and Boo Radley, Scout and Jem are forced to confront racism, injustice, and other painful realities of their society.

Publication history

To Kill a Mockingbird was published on July 11, 1960. Critics gave the novel mixed reviews. A critic for the *Atlantic Monthly* called the work "pleasant, undemanding reading." Another reviewer complained that the novel's two stories did not fit together.

An equal number of reviews, however, heaped praise on the novel. Many complimented Lee's storytelling and characters that were "beautifully, even profoundly, realized." Lee dazzled one critic with her portrayal of children: "[Scout's] dramatic recital of the joys, fears, dreams, misdemeanors, and problems of her little circle of friends and enemies gives the most vivid, realistic, and delightful portrayal of a child's world ever presented by an American novelist, with the possible exception of Mark Twain's *Tom Sawyer* and *Huckleberry Finn.*"

The reading public also embraced *To Kill a Mockingbird*. During its first year of publication, the novel sold half a million copies. By the end of the following year, it had gone through fourteen printings and sold more than two and a half million copies.

Lee was clearly a talented writer, but she had also written a novel whose themes of racism and injustice were very timely. As Lee finished her manuscript, the civil rights movement had begun the struggle against racial inequality and injustice.

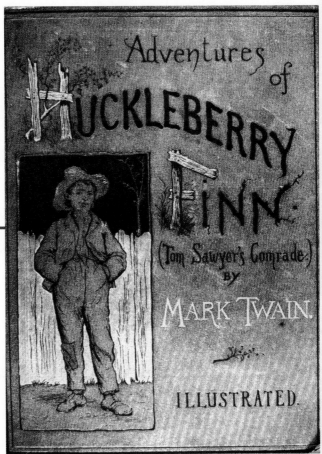

Many reviewers have compared Lee's novel to the work of other great authors who wrote about the South, such as Mark Twain. Horton Foote, who wrote the screenplay for the movie version of *To Kill a Mockingbird*, once explained how interested he became in the similarities between Lee's novel and *The Adventures of Huckleberry Finn*.

Slavery in the United States

Race relations in the United States grew out of a system of slavery. This system began when white Europeans enslaved black Africans and sent them to the Carribean and Brazil. The slave trade lasted from the early 1500s to the mid-1800s. During that time, traders enslaved around twelve million Africans and shipped them to the Americas.

The first Africans arrived in what would eventually become the United States in 1619. By the end of the American Revolution (1775–1783), the total black population numbered about 567,000. Most worked as slaves on large Southern **plantations**. In the years following the Revolution, most Northern states outlawed slavery. One reason was that slavery was not practical on small family farms in the region. Even so, slavery continued to spread in the South.

As the United States gained more territory, it added new states to the **Union**. The South wanted slavery to be legal in these new states, but the North wanted new states to be free. In 1820, lawmakers from the two regions made one of the first major political bargains to deal with this problem—the **Missouri Compromise**. Eventually, however, the North and South could no longer settle their differences through political agreements. After a series of crises, the two sides went to war.

THE MIDDLE PASSAGE

The diagram above shows how slave traders packed Africans onto their ships for the Middle Passage—the voyage between Africa and the slave colonies in the Americas. Ship captains had an interest in loading as many Africans onto their vessels as possible. They crammed the branded and chained captives into quarters with hardly enough space to sit up or turn over. Even though conditions were inhuman, traders made an effort—through forced feedings, for example—to see that their precious cargo survived the voyage. Even so, an estimated ten to twenty percent of the captives died during the Middle Passage.

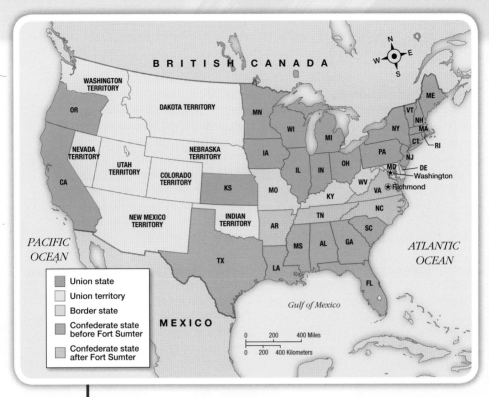

This map shows the states that remained faithful to the Union and those that joined the Confederacy during the Civil War.

Civil War

Agreements failed after Abraham Lincoln won the 1860 presidential election. He and his party were against the expansion of slavery. Southern states began to withdraw from the Union to protect their right to own slaves. These states then joined together as the "**Confederate States of America (CSA)**."

The memory of this period is still strong in Maycomb. On Scout's first day of school, students find out that their teacher is from Winston County. Winston County became famous during the Civil War because it was not willing to support the Confederacy. "When Alabama seceded [withdrew] from the Union on January 11, 1861," explains Scout, "Winston County seceded from Alabama, and every child in Maycomb County knew it."

The Civil War began on April 12, 1861, after Confederate forces fired on **Fort Sumter**, South Carolina. The fighting went on for four years. By the time the conflict ended, nearly 2.5 million soldiers had fought. More than 620,000 had lost their lives.

The South officially surrendered on April 9, 1865, in the small Virginia town of Appomattox, Court House. Many of Maycomb's citizens still feel the sting of this surrender. When the town experiences its first snowfall since the surrender, the Finch's neighbor, Mr. Avery, blames Jem and Scout for the event: " 'See what you've done?' he said. 'Hasn't snowed in Maycomb since Appomattox. It's bad children like you makes the seasons change.' "

Abolishing slavery

The full name of the character Bob Ewell is Robert E. Lee Ewell. This is significant because General Robert E. Lee (of whom Harper Lee herself is said to be a distant relation) was the Commanding General of the Confederate Army of Northern Virginia. At Appomattox, Lee surrendered to Ulysses Grant, General-in-Chief of all United States forces.

The surrender finally brought an end to slavery in the United States. During the Civil War, President Lincoln had issued the Emancipation Proclamation. This act freed slaves in Confederate territory. In January of 1865, Lincoln urged Congress to end slavery throughout the country. The **13th Amendment**, which abolished slavery, was approved by the end of the year.

Slavery had become illegal, but it would take the nation a long time to adjust to this change. As slavery had taken root in the Americas, millions of people had come to associate slavery with African Americans. They then began to think of being black as a sign of inferiority. This deep-rooted racism would poison relations between African Americans and whites for a long time to come. Lee shows the lingering effects of this poison in the fictional town of Maycomb.

Robert E. Lee (1807–1870)

Robert E. Lee was born into an important Virginia family and did very well as a student at the U.S. Military Academy at West Point. Lee did not want to fight the Union. He felt, however, that he must stand by his native Virginia. About this decision, Lee later said, "I did only what my duty demanded. I could have taken no other course without dishonor." Lee's military genius was a major factor in keeping the Confederacy alive for the four years of the Civil War.

After the Civil War, racist white southerners formed terrorist groups, such as the Ku Klux Klan, to maintain white supremacy. This 1874 cartoon by Thomas Nast illustrates the horrors that African Americans faced in the Reconstruction South.

Reconstruction

After the war, the federal government brought the former Confederate states back into the Union. This process, called Reconstruction, was difficult. The war had devastated the South, and a labor force of four million slaves was now "technically" free. As Scout explains, "the disturbance between the North and the South [. . .] left [her ancestors] stripped of everything but their land."

The federal government passed civil rights acts to safeguard the newly freed slaves. In addition, the nation ratified the **14th and 15th Amendments**, also intended to protect civil rights. Congress imposed military rule over the South to see that the region cooperated.

Many white southerners resisted the new policies. States passed Black Codes—laws intended to maintain **white supremacy** and restrict the

freedom of former slaves. White people also organized secret groups, such as the **Ku Klux Klan** (KKK) and the **Knights of the White Camellia**, to terrorize freed slaves. Federal troops tried to stop such activities, but they had little success.

In Chapter 11, Mrs. Dubose (who is said to keep a Confederate pistol under her pillow) upsets Jem by insulting Atticus. She says, "Your father's no better than the **niggers** and trash he works for." Jem fights back by destroying a section of Mrs. Dubose's garden where white camellias grow.

By the 1870s, opponents of Reconstruction had regained control of most southern states. The surviving Reconstruction governments fell not long after the 1876 presidential election. By April 1877, the last federal troops had departed.

Jim Crow

African Americans faced many challenges during Reconstruction. Even so, the freed slaves made extraordinary progress. Many African-American communities started their own schools and churches. The congregation to which Calpurnia belongs named its church First Purchase "because it was paid for from the first earnings of freed slaves." These communities also elected a large number of African Americans to federal and state office.

After federal troops left the South, discrimination against African Americans increased. Gradually, a system of racial segregation known as **Jim Crow** began to take hold. Jim Crow takes its name from a character in a popular **minstrel** show. The character represented African Americans as inferior.

By the beginning of the 1900s, Jim Crow came to refer to the body of racist laws and actions that denied African Americans their civil rights. The Jim Crow system survived into the 1950s, when the civil rights movement began to bring it to an end.

By 1910, every state of the former Confederacy had adopted laws that segregated spaces where African Americans and whites might be together. Jim Crow laws affected railroad cars, buses, schools, hospitals, churches, parks, theaters, restaurants, restrooms, water fountains, and even cemeteries. The South also passed laws that made it nearly impossible for African Americans to vote.

Under segregation, blacks and whites had to use separate facilities. In this photo an African-American man leaves the "**Colored** Waiting Room" at the Trailway Bus Terminal in Jackson, Mississippi.

16

The Jim Crow South received support from the federal government. In 1896, the U.S. **Supreme Court** decided that as long as the facilities were equal, states could have separate facilities for blacks and whites. But facilities were grossly unequal. For example, governments gave far less funding, if any, to public schools for blacks than they gave to white schools. Even so, those who were concerned by these inequalities were in no position to enforce the law.

Jim Crow in Maycomb

Maycomb's blacks are observing Jim Crow laws when they sit in the courthouse balcony during the Robinson trial. Segregation laws would have forbade their sitting below with the whites. Jim Crow also led to the segregation of black and white residential areas in southern towns. In Maycomb, the black community is called the "Quarters." Many whites were totally against black education. Calpurnia had to teach her son Zeebo at home by reading to him from the Bible and law books.

W. E. B. Du Bois took part in the creation of the National Association for the Advancement of Colored People (NAACP) in 1909. The NAACP is a civil rights organization that was formed to secure political, educational, social, and economic equality for African Americans.

Double consciousness

In his 1903 book, *The Souls of Black Folk*, W. E. B. Du Bois described a split in the way African Americans thought of themselves. Du Bois believed that the history of race relations in the United States stopped blacks from thinking of themselves just as Americans. The past forced blacks to also look at themselves through the eyes of the dominant whites.

Du Bois described this split as "a peculiar sensation, this double-**consciousness**, this sense of always looking at one's self through the eyes of others [. . .] One ever feels his twoness,—an American, a Negro; two souls, two thoughts [. . .]"

To Kill a Mockingbird captures this "twoness" in the scene that takes place in Calpurnia's church. Jem and Scout wonder why Calpurnia has one way of speaking in their home and another in the Quarters. During their visit, Scout asks Calpurnia, "Why do you talk nigger-talk to the—to your folks when you know it's not right?" Calpurnia's two ways of behaving made Scout think: "That Calpurnia led a modest double life never dawned on me. The idea that she had a separate existence outside our household was a novel one, to say nothing of her having command of two languages."

Wearing the mask

This double life was a necessity under Jim Crow. Outside of their own communities, African Americans had to follow special rules of behavior. Whites expected blacks to turn their eyes down in their presence and to wait until they were spoken to before speaking. Even African Americans who could afford them avoided luxuries, such as fancy clothes and expensive cars, so as not to stand out.

In his poem "We Wear the Mask" Paul Laurence Dunbar describes the **strategies** African Americans had to develop to survive in such an atmosphere. These strategies also had to be adopted by whites who violated Jim Crow ideas. This is illustrated in Scout and Dill's encounter with a white man named Dolphus Raymond.

Raymond married and had children with a black woman. To give the community a way of explaining how this could possibly have happened, Raymond pretends to be a drunk. He staggers around with a paper bag that people assume contains liquor. He confesses to Scout and Dill that the bag actually contains soda pop. Such strategies may seem unusual today, but those who lived under Jim Crow took them very seriously.

Paul Laurence Dunbar (left) published the poem "We Wear the Mask" in his *Lyrics of Lowly Life* in 1896.

WE WEAR THE MASK

We wear the mask that grins and lies,
It hides our cheeks and shades our eyes,—
This debt we pay to human guile;
With torn and bleeding hearts we smile,
And mouth with myriad subtleties.

Why should the world be over-wise,
In counting all our tears and sighs?
Nay, let them only see us, while
We wear the mask.

We smile, but O great Christ, our cries
To thee from tortured souls arise.
We sing, but oh the clay is vile
Beneath our feet, and along the mile;
But let the world dream otherwise,
We wear the mask!

Lynching

People who violated the laws and ideas of the Jim Crow system faced harsh penalties—including beatings, mutilation, and death. In the 1860s and 1870s, terrorist organizations such as the KKK had brutalized and killed hundreds of African Americans. But the situation got worse after 1877.

In the 1880s, an outbreak of **lynchings** began in the United States. The lynchings became so widespread that Mark Twain published an essay in 1901 entitled "The United States of Lyncherdom." Most lynching victims were southern black men.

Violence against African Americans was not new, but the nature of the violence had changed. After the 1890s, lynch mobs began to torture, **dismember**, and even barbecue their victims. Whites collected and sold victims' body parts as souvenirs. Newspapers ran advertisements for lynchings. White parents even brought their children to lynchings.

These practices were still common in the 1930s, which saw 130 recorded lynchings. "Why reasonable people go stark raving mad when anything involving a Negro comes up," Atticus admits, "is something I don't pretend to understand." Harper Lee became aware of this madness at an early age. She probably thought about such experiences when she wrote the tragic story of Tom Robinson.

Between 1882 and 1968, there were 4,742 recorded lynchings of African Americans. The 1930 lynching of Thomas Shipp and Abram Smith (seen left) took place in Marion, Indiana. The victims of most lynchings, however, were southern black men. Many white people collected and traded photographs of lynchings that were printed as postcards.

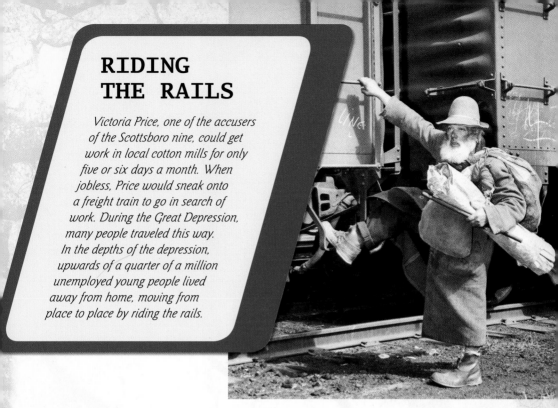

Scottsboro Case

The story of Tom Robinson has similarities with incidents that occurred in Lee's native Alabama. Among these is the Scottsboro case, which started when Lee was about five years old.

The Scottsboro case began on March 25, 1931. A group of young white and black men were riding the rails (see box above) from Tennessee to Alabama. On the journey, the black men fought with the white men and threw them off the train. An armed group organized by a local sheriff met the train in Paint Rock, Alabama. They found nine black youths and two white women—Victoria Price and Ruby Bates. All of them were taken to the county jail in Scottsboro.

Perhaps fearing that they would face jail time for **vagrancy**, the two women accused the youths of rape. They probably expected that officials would be more lenient toward the victims of such a crime. Word of these accusations soon spread. As on the eve of Tom Robinson's trial, an armed mob began to gather outside the Scottsboro jail. The mob aimed to lynch the nine suspects, but it dispersed when the **National Guard** arrived.

The first of many trials in the Scottsboro case began on April 6, 1931. Three days later, despite testimony by doctors that no rape had occurred, an all-white jury convicted the nine youths. All but the youngest received a death sentence. Then began a long series of appeals and retrials. Juries continued to deliver guilty verdicts, even after Ruby Bates said that she and Victoria had made up the rape story.

At the time of their arrest, almost all of the "Scottsboro nine" (shown here in 1933) were teenagers. One was just twelve years old, another was disabled, another was nearly blind, and all were illiterate. Only four of the young men knew each other at the time of their arrest.

Justice at last

In 1937, Alabama finally freed the four youngest Scottsboro defendants. They had been in prison for six years. In the following years, Alabama **paroled** all but one of the defendants. The last, Haywood Patterson, escaped from prison in 1948—a year before Lee left law school.

Scottsboro and Maycomb

The Scottsboro case has many parallels with Tom Robinson's story. Both cases involve the **alleged** rape of white women. Both occurred in Alabama during the Great Depression, and in both, African-American males were the defendants.

Some of those involved in the Scottsboro case, like Atticus, showed great courage in seeking justice for the defendants. Judge James E. Horton, for example, presided over the 1933 trial of Patterson. Judge Horton actually "set aside" a jury's conviction of Patterson, saying it was not justified by the evidence.

The testimony of doctors is also an issue in both trials. Physicians in the Scottsboro case found no evidence that a rape had occurred. During Robinson's trial, Atticus points out that no doctors were called to the scene of the crime, and no medical examination took place afterward.

Sadly, the injustice of the Scottsboro case—reflected in the Robinson trial—was not unusual. African Americans were used to receiving unequal treatment from the U.S. legal system. Many years would pass before this changed.

The Civil Rights Movement

It was not until the 1950s that Jim Crow became fragile. Lawyers for the National Association for the Advancement of Colored People (NAACP) began arguments in May 1954, in front of the Supreme Court in the case of *Brown v. Board of Education*. They tried to persuade the nine justices that the segregation of public schools deprived black children of the "equal protection of the laws." The 14th Amendment, passed during Reconstruction, promises that protection.

On May 17, 1954, the court ruled unanimously that segregation in public education was illegal. The justices agreed that segregation had a harmful effect on minority children because the children viewed it as a sign of inferiority.

The court's decision only applied to public schools, but many believed this case would bring an end to all forms of segregation. However, in May 1955 the court issued a follow-up decision known as *Brown II*. In *Brown II*, the court ordered schools to desegregate "with all deliberate speed." The justices realized that many communities would resist its decision, and they deliberately used this phrase to give school districts more time to make changes. Not long after *Brown II*, a terrible crime brought an end to African Americans' patience for this kind of delay.

Linda Brown Smith (on the left) was nine years old in this 1952 photo with her sister Terri Lynn. She was in the third grade when her father, Oliver Brown, and thirteen other parents in Topeka, Kansas, filed a lawsuit against Topeka's Board of Education. The Supreme Court combined the Topeka case with four others from around the nation before ruling in May 1954 that segregation in public schools was unconstitutional.

23

Emmett Till in 1955, just prior to his murder. He was buried on September 6, 1955. Before the burial, as many as 50,000 mourners passed by the open casket. Many people were reduced to tears or fainting at the sight and smell of the mutilated body.

The murder of Emmett Till

In August 1955, fourteen-year-old Emmett Till left his home in Chicago to spend the summer holiday with his great uncle in Money, Mississippi. His family had warned him about Southern racism, but Emmett did not really understand the rigid boundaries of Jim Crow.

On the evening of August 24, Emmett was playing with his cousins and some other kids outside of Bryant's Grocery and Meat Market. Perhaps on a dare from one of the boys, Emmett whistled at Carolyn Bryant, the white woman who was working the counter. Word of what Emmett had done soon spread through the community.

Carolyn Bryant's husband, Roy Bryant, heard what happened when he returned from a trip three days later. He was furious. At around 2:30 a.m. on Sunday, August 28, Bryant and his half-brother, J. W. Milam, went to the home of Emmett's great uncle. They woke Emmett up and took him away in their car. That was the last time anyone saw Emmett alive.

Three days later, a fisherman found Emmett's mangled body in the Tallahatchie River. A 75-pound (34-kilogram) **cotton gin** fan was tied around his neck with barbed wire. Kidnapping charges, which authorities had already brought against Bryant and Milam, were upgraded to murder.

The killers go free

After the body was found, Emmett's mother, Mamie Till Mobley, insisted that his body be brought back to Chicago. After seeing her son's mutilated body, she decided to have an open-casket funeral and to allow photographers to take pictures of her son. "I think everybody needed to know what had happened to Emmett Till," she said.

At the funeral on September 6, 1955, tens of thousands of mourners walked by Emmett's coffin. Thousands more gasped in horror when they saw photos of the disfigured corpse in that month's issue of *Jet* magazine.

There was plenty of evidence to prove that Bryant and Milam were guilty. Even so, an all-white jury **acquitted** the two men on September 23. The jury had met for just over an hour. Afterward, one of the jurors reported that it only took that long because they stopped to have a soda pop. They wanted to stretch things out and make it look good.

As in the Scottsboro case, there are several similarities between the cases of Till and Robinson. Till's actions went against the taboo prohibiting contact between black men and white women. Once again, an all-white jury had failed to uphold justice.

J. W. Milam (left) and Roy Bryant celebrate with their wives after being acquitted of Till's murder. In January 1956, *Look* magazine published "The Shocking Story of Approved Killing in Mississippi." In the article, Milam and Bryant talk in detail about how they murdered Emmett Till.

A different time

The grief and outrage caused by the murder of Emmett Till spurred many civil rights **activists** into action. They saw that the legal system alone would not bring an end to racial injustice. Change required action both inside and outside the courts.

In December 1955, just three months after Emmett's burial, Rosa Parks boarded a bus in Montgomery, Alabama. After taking her seat, the driver told Rosa to stand up and give her seat to a white man. Her refusal led to the Montgomery Bus **Boycott**, which protested the segregation of public buses. It was one of the first major protests of the civil rights movement. Rosa said that Emmett Till was on her mind when she refused to give up her seat.

The boycott ended a year later. The courts ruled that Montgomery's segregated busing was unconstitutional. The success of the boycott was an encouragement to the movement. In protest after protest, civil rights activists began to tear down the system of Jim Crow:

- September 1957: President Eisenhower sends federal troops to Little Rock, Arkansas. The troops enforce the court-ordered desegregation of Little Rock Central High School after defiance from Orval Faubus, Arkansas State Governor.
- February 1960: African-American college students organize "**sit-ins**" in Greensboro, North Carolina. They aim to integrate city facilities.

Martin Luther King Jr. (1929–1968)

Martin Luther King was a Baptist minister and an important civil rights activist. He is seen here, arrested for loitering near a courtroom where one of his fellow activists was on trial in Montgomery, 1958. He came to prominence after taking a leadership role during the Montgomery Bus Boycott. King was an important promoter of nonviolence. In 1963, he helped to organize the March on Washington, at which he delivered his famous "I Have a Dream" speech. During his speech, King expressed his hope for the future: "I have a dream that my four little children will one day live in a nation where they will not be judged by the color of their skin, but by the content of their character." King was assassinated in 1968, just four years after winning the

- May 1961: Civil rights activists organize "**Freedom Rides**" to **integrate** interstate bus facilities.
- April 1963: Large protests, in which children participate, take place in Birmingham. National television stations show Birmingham police using fire hoses and police dogs on protesters.
- August 28, 1963: On a date chosen in memory of Emmett Till's murder, a quarter of a million people march to Washington, D.C., where Martin Luther King delivers his famous speech, "I Have a Dream."

The movement's victories

Civil rights protests soon convinced the government of the need for action. Federal and state officials began to enforce existing civil rights laws, such as the 14th Amendment. Activists also won further safeguards for civil rights. These included the **Civil Rights Act of 1964**, the **24th Amendment**, and the **Voting Rights Act** of 1965.

It was just as the civil rights movement was heating up that Lee was writing *To Kill a Mockingbird*. During that time, Lee made frequent trips between New York and Alabama, an important center of the movement. It is curious that Lee decided not to place her characters—who confront the evils of racism and injustice—in a **contemporary** setting. Instead, she chose the time of the Great Depression.

In 1963, organizers for the Southern Christian Leadership Conference began to recruit children to join a civil rights protest in Birmingham, Alabama. Many were outraged when they saw the confrontations between children and Birmingham police on national television. In the photo below, the children who had participated in the protests wait to be taken to jail by a police van.

Childhood and the Past
in *To Kill a Mockingbird*

The Great Depression began in October 1929 with the collapse of the U.S. **stock market**. The collapse sent the economy into a crisis. Hundreds of banks went out of business, more than 90,000 businesses failed, and millions lost their jobs. The economic crisis began in the United States, but it spread quickly throughout the industrial world.

The Depression hit the South especially hard because they had already experienced decades of economic depression. The southern economy depended on agriculture. The prices of agricultural products dropped to levels not seen since the Civil War, over sixty years before. Maycomb's farmers felt the impact of the price drop. On her first day of school, Atticus tells Scout that the Cunninghams "are country folks, farmers, and the crash hit them hardest." Later, Scout explains why Atticus is called to an emergency legislative session: "There were **sit-down strikes** in Birmingham; **bread lines** in the cities grew longer, people in the country grew poorer."

GREAT DEPRESSION IN ALABAMA

The Great Depression had a lasting impact on children, especially those whose parents had lost their jobs. Some children left school to work so that they could help their parents pay for food and shelter. Many schools had to close down. Others had to make do with fewer resources. This photo, taken around 1937 (when Lee was about eleven years old) shows children in a Scottsboro, Alabama schoolhouse. According to Lee's close friends, the depression had a strong impact on her. Even the income from a successful novel has not changed Lee's habit of being very careful with money. "She was raised in the Depression in a little Alabama town, and she still has that sensibility."

One New Deal program was the WPA's Federal Art Project. Artists who joined the project created thousands of works of art. Many of the project's murals still decorate public buildings in the United States. This 1942 mural, located in the Department of the Interior building, shows a large crowd at the Lincoln Memorial. The work commemorates a concert given by the African-American singer Marian Anderson on Easter Sunday, April 1939.

The New Deal

By the time of the 1932 presidential election, approximately thirteen million people were unemployed. The U.S. people wanted a president who would act boldly to end their suffering. They elected Franklin Delano Roosevelt. During his campaign, Roosevelt promised a "**New Deal**" for Americans. The New Deal became the name of the programs and policies that Roosevelt used to fight the Depression.

When Atticus discusses the Cunninghams with Scout, he says, "If he held his mouth right, Mr. Cunningham could get a WPA job, but his land would go to ruin if he left it [. . .]" The WPA was Roosevelt's Works Progress Administration. This New Deal program helped jobless people keep their self-respect by giving them useful work.

The National Industrial Recovery Act was another New Deal program. It was passed by President Roosevelt in 1933 and helped businesses during the Great Depression. But at the end of *To Kill a Mockingbird*, Scout notices that, "People had removed from their store windows and automobiles the stickers that said NRA—WE DO OUR PART. I asked Atticus why, and he said it was because the National Recovery Act was dead. I asked who killed it; he said nine old men." The "nine old men" are the nine justices of the U.S. Supreme Court, who, in 1935, declared the act invalid.

The moral strength of *To Kill a Mockingbird*

At a time when the civil rights movement was heating up, Lee chose to write a novel about racism and injustice that is narrated by a child during the Great Depression. This was surely a deliberate strategy on Lee's part.

Had she chosen to place her characters and stories in the same era as the civil rights movement, it is unlikely that Lee's novel would have had the same power. The civil rights movement brought out strong emotions in the American people. For many, it would have been difficult to reflect honestly on racism and injustice had those ideas been presented in that time period.

Addressing the issues from a historical perspective and through the innocent eyes of a child helps to give *To Kill a Mockingbird* its great moral strength. Lee allows readers to think about these difficult issues from a distance.

Dealing with problems from a distance

On the one hand, there is the **psychological** distance that separates adulthood from childhood. Looking through the eyes of a child forces people to think differently. The freshness and purity of a child's perspective is shown, for example, in the scene in which Jem hears the jury find Tom Robinson guilty (see pages 39–41).

THE CLARKS' DOLLS

Encouraging adults to see through the eyes of children was also a strategy of the NAACP lawyers in Brown v. Board of Education. During their arguments before the Supreme Court, the lawyers cited research by psychologists Kenneth and Mamie Phipps Clark. The Clarks found that African-American children overwhelmingly believed white dolls were nicer and prettier than black dolls. The children also said that the black dolls were bad. This disturbing evidence helped the justices to understand the serious damage caused by segregation and racism. The photo above is taken from the article "Breeding a Color Bar?" published in Picture Post in 1952, and illustrating the Clarks' findings.

On the other hand, there is also the historical distance that separates the present from the past. Thinking about racism in history is sometimes easier than thinking about racism in the present. Reading about how Eleanor Roosevelt worked for racial equality in the 1930s might be the first step for some readers in reconsidering their own ideas about race today.

In this way, Lee makes the reader a little like Scout when she eavesdrops on her uncle and father discussing racism and the Robinson trial. At the end of their conversation, after she is found out, Scout says, "I never figured out how Atticus knew I was listening, and it was not until many years later that I realized he wanted me to hear every word he said." Many readers become so engrossed in Lee's skillful storytelling that they do not realize until much later the strong impact the novel has had on their outlook and opinions.

World War II

Roosevelt's New Deal provided much-needed relief during the Depression. But the New Deal did not end the Depression. War ended the Depression. World War II began in 1939 and lasted until 1945. When the United States began to supply materials for the war effort, the nation's economy finally started to grow again.

Eleanor Roosevelt (1884–1962)

*Eleanor Roosevelt (seen here in July 1933) was first lady from 1933 until 1945. As first lady she worked hard to promote equality for all Americans. In 1934, for example, she arranged for the president to meet with the NAACP to discuss anti-lynching legislation. Such activities make her an object of scorn in Maycomb. At Aunt Alexandra's "**missionary** tea" Mrs. Merriweather gossips about a visit that Eleanor Roosevelt made to Alabama. At a meeting of the Southern Conference for Human Welfare in Birmingham (which actually took place in 1939), the First Lady sat with a group of African Americans. After state authorities told her that she was violating segregation laws, she sat down in the center aisle, between whites and African Americans. "I think that woman, that Mrs. Roosevelt's lost her mind," says Mrs. Merriweather, "—just plain lost her mind coming down to Birmingham and tryin' to sit with 'em."*

Nazism

World War II started after Germany, under Adolf Hitler, invaded Poland. Hitler was head of Germany's **Nazi Party**. He became the leader of the German government in 1933. Soon, he began to rule as a **dictator**. In his rise to political power, Hitler declared the superiority of the German race. Hitler blamed Germany's Jews for the nation's problems since its defeat in World War I (1914–1918) and for its suffering during the Great Depression.

Frightening similarities

After taking power in 1933, the Nazis began an assault on the Jewish population. They called on people to boycott Jewish businesses. They dismissed Jews from government positions, and they limited Jews' ability to go to schools. In September 1935, the Nazis passed the **Nuremberg Laws**. These measures stripped Jews of German citizenship. They also prohibited marriage and sexual relations between Jews and Germans.

1936 BERLIN OLYMPICS

At the 1936 Summer Olympics in Berlin, Germany, the track-and-field athlete Jesse Owens won four gold medals. Here, he salutes his victory in the long jump (center), for which he set a new Olympic record. Germany's Luz Long (right) gives a Nazi salute. The African-American Owens upset Adolf Hitler's plan to use the games to demonstrate Aryan supremacy. Aryan was a word used by the Nazis to identify a supposed "master race" of white-North European descent.

During World War II, the Nazi's built death camps, such as Auschwitz in German-occupied Poland, solely for the purpose of murdering civilians. It is thought that more than a million people were killed at Auschwitz. Poison gas chambers at the camp could hold 2,000 people at a time. With such facilities, Nazis could gas and incinerate 12,000 human beings each day.

The Nuremberg Laws were passed just as Scout and Jem returned to school in the autumn of 1935. At a weekly "current events period," one of Scout's classmates summarizes an article he has read about Nazi Germany: "Adolf Hitler has been after the Jews and he's puttin' 'em in prisons and he's taking away all their property and he won't let any of 'em out of the country and he's washin' all the feeble-minded and [. . . he's also] started a program to round up all the half Jews too and he wants to register 'em in case they might wanta cause him any trouble and I think this is a bad thing and that's my current event."

Discovering hypocrisy

The students ask how such injustice could be possible. Their teacher, Miss Gates, explains that the United States is "a **democracy** and Germany is a **dictatorship** [. . .] Over here we don't believe in persecuting anybody. Persecution comes from people who are prejudiced."

Scout is puzzled, since she recalls remarks that Miss Gates made at the Robinson trial: "I heard her say it's time somebody taught 'em a lesson, they were gettin' way above themselves, an' the next thing they think they can do is marry us." Unsettled by Miss Gates's **hypocrisy**, Scout asks Jem "how can you hate Hitler so bad an' then turn around and be ugly about folks right at home?"

Lee again gives readers the space to make their own moral judgments. *To Kill a Mockingbird* was published fifteen years after the end of World War II. So, unlike Scout and her teacher, readers know that the Nazis eventually murdered eleven million men, women, and children—including an estimated six million Jews.

The Mockingbird Theme

Racism and injustice are major issues in *To Kill a Mockingbird*. But Lee explores other issues, including education, religion, the role of the family, and what it means to be a woman. She explores all these issues together, in common concern for all of society's most vulnerable members.

The title of Lee's novel emphasizes the importance of this theme. Early in the novel, Miss Maudie tells Scout that "Mockingbirds [see page 43] don't do one thing but make music for us to enjoy [. . .] they don't do one thing but sing their hearts out for us. That's why it's a sin to kill a mockingbird." For Lee, mockingbirds represent weak and defenseless people—especially children and the victims of prejudice and racism.

CORPORAL PUNISHMENT

During her first day in school, Scout's teacher hits her with a ruler. Corporal punishment, or punishment by physical pain, is illegal in many countries. But many U.S. states, including Alabama, still permits paddling and other physical punishments in 2006.

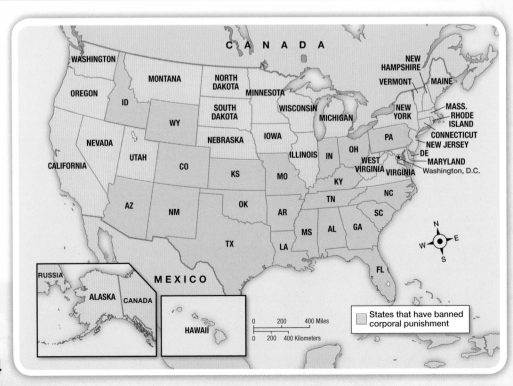

Scout goes to school

In passages about Scout's education, Lee shows her concern for children who might be harmed by the attitudes and behavior of their teachers. When Scout's first-grade teacher discovers that Scout can read, she tells Scout to tell her father not to teach her anymore, "It's best to begin reading with a fresh mind." You tell him I'll take over from here and try to undo the damage [. . .] Your father does not know how to teach. You can have a seat now."

Lee clearly has a passion for learning and education. This is evident in passages describing Jem, Scout, and Dill's love of children's literature. It is also evident when Lee describes the lessons that Atticus and Calpurnia taught the children.

It is also clear that Lee has a critical view of the way education is practiced in the public schools. After her first year in school, Scout reflects: "I could not help receiving the impression that I was being cheated out of something. Out of what I knew not, yet I did not believe that twelve years of unrelieved boredom was exactly what the state had in mind for me."

Religious practice

Lee is also concerned with the effects of religious practice. Lee herself is a lifelong member of Monroeville's First United Methodist Church. She is someone who takes religion very seriously. Even so, she is as critical of religion, as practiced, as she is of education.

Lee is particularly troubled by religious extremism, especially the effects such extremism has on vulnerable characters such as Boo Radley. Referring to Boo's very religious family, Miss Maudie tells Scout: "There are just some kind of men who—who're so busy worrying about the next world they've never learned to live in this one, and you can look down the street [to the Radley's] and see the results."

Richard Allen (1760–1831)

Calpurnia's church, First Purchase, belongs to the African Methodist Episcopal Church. The church developed from a Philadelphia congregation that withdrew from another church in 1787 because of racial discrimination. Though the church originated in the North, it spread rapidly in the South after the Civil War. Richard Allen (shown here) became the denomination's first bishop in 1816.

This painting is *Crimson Rambler,* by Philip Leslie Hale. It portrays a refined lady of the South. Aunt Alexandra presses Scout to adopt the role of the southern lady—to become more delicate, feminine, refined, and charming.

The impurity of women

Scout senses that certain aspects of her own religious upbringing might not be so healthy. When she and Jem go to Calpurnia's church, Scout disagrees with Reverend Sykes's **sermon**. He focusses too much on the faults of women: "Again, as I had often met it in my own church, I was confronted with the **Impurity of Women doctrine** that seemed to preoccupy all clergymen."

The way young girls should behave

Church is not the only place where Scout has to deal with ideas about women. Throughout the novel, Scout gets advice about how young ladies should or should not behave.

The pressure on Scout to act like a lady gets stronger when her aunt moves in on the eve of the Robinson trial.

When Scout asks about the purpose of her visit, Aunt Alexandra explains that she and Atticus "decided that it would be best for you to have some feminine influence. It won't be many years, Jean Louise, before you become interested in clothes and boys." She was determined to bring about a change in the way Scout dressed and behaved: "Aunt Alexandra was fanatical on the subject of my attire. I could not possibly hope to be a lady if I wore breeches; when I said I could do nothing in a dress, she said I wasn't supposed to be doing things that required pants."

The care and advice that Scout receives from her father helps her to deal with such demands. When Scout tells him that Aunt Alexandra wants her to "behave like a sunbeam," Atticus says that there are "already enough sunbeams in the family and to go on about my business, he didn't mind me much the way I was."

With the arrival of her Aunt Alexandra, Scout

> **felt the starched walls of a pink cotton penitentiary closing in on me.**

Black men and white women

Lee also criticizes traditional ideas about women in the story of Tom Robinson. In some ways, Mayella Ewell is also one of the novel's mockingbirds. Society's ideas about race and the role of women trap her into accusing Robinson of rape, and the consequences are deadly.

In the United States, close contact between whites and African Americans was taboo for centuries. In a 1947 study, a **sociologist** asked white southerners to say what they thought African Americans most wanted by demanding their civil rights. The number one response was intermarriage and sexual relations with whites. African Americans knew that many white people feared this. African-American men in the Jim Crow South didn't dare look at, or accidentally touch, white women.

Ida B. Wells-Barnett (1862–1931)

Ida B. Wells-Barnett (seen here circa 1890s) provides a different model of "southern womanhood." Wells-Barnett grew up in Mississippi. After going to college, she took a job teaching in Memphis, Tennessee, and became a co-owner of the Memphis newspaper **Free Speech**. *After a mob lynched three of her friends in 1892, she began to use the paper to campaign against lynching. Her outspokenness brought threats to her own life, and she was forced to move. She eventually settled in Chicago. Wells-Barnett continued her campaign for racial equality and, with W. E. B. Du Bois, was one of the original founders of the NAACP. She died in March 1931.*

37

RACE MIXING

In Chapter 16, readers are introduced to Dolphus Raymond, who married an African-American woman and had children with her. Raymond's marriage violated Alabama laws forbidding interracial marriage or sex. Violators faced up to seven years in prison. The interracial marriage struggle continued for many years across the United States. Mr. and Mrs. Richard Perry Loving (below), an interracial couple, fought Virginia's law against interracial marriages in 1965. Alabama's law was not taken off the books until November 2000, 33 years after the U.S. Supreme Court declared such laws unconstitutional. Even then, nearly 40 percent of Alabamans voted to keep the ban.

A different model

After the *Brown* decision, some white people still feared that white women were not safe around African-American men. Alabama Senator Walter C. Givhan said, "What is the real purpose of this? To open the bedroom doors of our white women to Negro men." At the missionary tea, Mrs. Farrow says it "looks like we're fighting a losing battle [. . .] We can educate 'em till we're blue in the face, we can try till we drop to make Christians out of 'em, but there's no lady safe in her bed these nights." Atticus is unique in being unwilling to preserve "the polite fiction [of Southern womanhood] at the expense of human life."

In Scout, Lee presents a different model of womanhood. By the novel's end, this model has begun to take shape. When Boo asks Scout to take him home, Scout puts her foot on the top step and stops. "I would lead him through our house, but I would never lead him home. 'Mr. Arthur [Boo], bend your arm down here, like that. That's right, sir.' I slipped my hand into the crook of his arm. He had to stoop a little to accommodate me, but if Miss Stephanie Crawford was watching from her upstairs window, she would see Arthur Radley escorting me down the sidewalk, as any gentleman would do." For Scout, being a lady means letting Boo feel like a gentleman.

Coming-of-Age

To Kill a Mockingbird fits the pattern, in many ways, of a "coming-of-age" novel. Such novels usually feature one or more characters who, like Scout and Jem, are in their **formative** years. Generally speaking, coming-of-age novels follow the moral, psychological, and spiritual growth of their main characters —usually from childhood to adulthood. Writers describe the factors that affect their characters' growth. These might include the characters' education, religion, or family life.

The adventures and experiences of the characters also affect their growth. Therefore, coming-of-age stories often describe characters' confrontations with hatred, love, sexuality, racism, death, or other realities of adult life.

Lee included many of these elements in *To Kill a Mockingbird*. The children experience and react to the influences of family life, education, and religion. They also confront the painful realities of racism and injustice in the story of Tom Robinson. Through these experiences the children begin their journey to maturity and adulthood.

Bildungsroman is a German word for a novel about a character's formative years. Many consider *Wilhelm Meister's Apprenticeship* to be the first novel of this type. It was written in 1795–1796 by the German author J. W. von Goethe (shown here in a 1786 painting by Tischbein).

This poster advertised the film adaptation of *To Kill a Mockingbird* (1962). In the book, two oak trees stand at the edge of the Radley property. During the summer of 1934, Boo leaves gifts for Jem and Scout in the knothole of one of the trees. Among the gifts were a medal, a pocket watch, a penknife, and figures carved out of soap, meant to represent the children.

Learning a "simple trick"

One of the ways in which the children mature is by following the advice that Atticus gives at the beginning of the novel. " 'If you can learn a simple trick,' Atticus tells Scout, 'you'll get along a lot better with all kinds of folks. You never really understand a person until you consider things from his point of view—[. . .] until you climb into his skin and walk around in it.' "

Jem seems to be capable of this trick already. He is ten years old at the start of the novel—four years older than Scout. Jem's ability is evident in the way he reacts to the injustices done to Boo Radley and Tom Robinson.

In Chapter 7, Nathan Radley cements in the hole in which Boo has been putting little toys for the children. Scout senses how deeply her brother feels this cruelty toward Boo: " ' [. . .] He stood there until nightfall, and I waited for him. When we went in the house I saw he had been crying; his face was dirty in the right places, but I thought it odd that I had not heard him."

Jem experiences the betrayal of Tom Robinson just as profoundly. In his innocence, Jem fully believes that the jury will find Robinson not guilty. During the final legal arguments, when Scout joins Jem in the balcony, Jem tells Scout " '[Atticus has] just gone over the evidence, [. . .] and we're gonna win, Scout. I don't see how we can't.' " Then, when the jury returns, we see how deeply the verdict wounds Jem. Scout describes what happens: "I shut my eyes. Judge Taylor was polling the jury: 'Guilty . . . guilty . . . guilty . . . guilty.' I peeked at Jem: his hands were white from gripping the balcony rail, and his shoulders jerked as if each 'guilty' was a separate stab between them."

Jem retreats into himself after that, trying to understand what has happened. Atticus tells Scout that, "Jem was trying hard to forget something, but what he was really doing was storing it away for a while, until enough time passed. Then he would be able to think about it and sort things out. When he was able to think about it, Jem would be himself again."

Actor Brock Peters (front right) played Tom Robinson in the 1962 film version of *To Kill a Mockingbird.* His powerful performance helped moviegoers understand the terrible injustices African Americans endured during the Jim Crow era. In the scene in which Atticus asks Robinson if he raped Mayella Ewell, Brock gives the tearful response: "I did not, sir." He delivered his lines so realistically that Gregory Peck, who played Atticus, (front left) admitted having to look away so that he too would not begin to cry. Peters passed away on August 23, 2005, at the age of 78.

During the early years of the civil rights movement, most protesters followed the principles of nonviolence. In this 1963 photograph, protesters are trying to integrate facilities in Jackson, Mississippi, by ordering meals at a lunch counter that refuses to serve African Americans. During their "sit-in," they bravely endure the abuse of whites.

Scout learns the trick

Scout does not share Jem's keen sense of **empathy** at the beginning of the novel. But with the love and guidance of her father and through the "classroom" of experience, Scout quickly matures. By the end of the novel she, too, can perform "the trick."

After Boo vanishes back into his home following the attack, Scout lingers on the porch and suddenly understands. "I turned to go home. Street lights winked down the street all the way to town. I had never seen our neighborhood from this angle." And then suddenly, she is in Boo's skin. In the passage that follows, Scout gazes down the street and begins to see the previous years' events from Boo's perspective: "Atticus was right. One time he said you never really know a man until you stand in his shoes and walk around in them. Just standing on the Radley porch was enough."

The growth of Atticus

Arguably, it is not only the children who are transformed by the events of *To Kill a Mockingbird*. One of the novel's most powerful passages suggests that Atticus Finch also undergoes a transformation.

At the end of the novel, Sheriff Heck Tate convinces Atticus that they should report that Bob Ewell died when he fell on his own knife. Both men know that Boo killed Ewell while defending the children. Even so, they work together to hide this fact. They know that revealing the details to the public would be extremely harmful to someone as shy as Boo.

Earlier in the novel, Atticus expressed a willingness, under unusual circumstances, to bend the law. But after the attack on his children, Atticus decides to break the law. This decision goes violently against the grain of Atticus' faith in the legal system.

Sparing a mockingbird

The passage in which Atticus makes his decision also reinforces the symbolic importance of the mockingbird theme. Atticus has already seen the sacrifice of Tom Robinson. He refuses to see Boo sacrificed as well. Scout understands her father's decision. She tells Atticus " 'Mr. Tate was right. Harming Boo Radley; Well it'd be sort of like shootin' a mockingbird, wouldn't it?' "

The growth of Atticus comes through his realization that he has placed too much faith in the legal system. At the end of the novel, Atticus decides that he must pursue justice both inside and outside of the courts. Lee has Atticus arrive at the same conclusion that thousands of civil rights activists were reaching as she wrote her novel. As one critic said of *To Kill a Mockingbird*: "Lee's novel ends where the civil rights movement begins."

Mockingbirds, which are especially common in the southern United States, are treasured for their beautiful songs. They are also famed for being able to imitate the sounds of other species. The song of the mockingbird is actually repeats of the calls of many other birds. Mockingbirds have even been known to imitate squeaky gates, pianos, sirens, and dogs. It is not uncommon for a mockingbird to have as many as 25 to 30 songs.

To Kill a Mockingbird Today

The popularity of *To Kill a Mockingbird* is as strong as ever. Since its publication in 1960, the novel has never been out of print. By 2000, *To Kill a Mockingbird* had sold more than thirty million copies.

Clearly, a major reason for the novel's popularity is that Lee is a talented writer and gifted storyteller. But the novel's moral qualities have also led to the book's success. Many of Lee's readers have talked about the moral impact the novel has had on their lives. Countless lawyers, for example, have said that the character of Atticus inspired their decision to go into law.

But the novel's moral impact extends beyond the legal community. In a 1991 "Survey of Lifetime Reading Habits," *To Kill a Mockingbird* was second only to the Bible in books that had made a difference in people's lives. In 2003, the American Film Institute chose Atticus as "the greatest hero in a hundred years of film history."

One writer has argued that "*To Kill a Mockingbird* became for the South of the 1960s what *Uncle Tom's Cabin* was to the North a hundred years earlier; a novel to change minds and arouse consciences [. . .] Harper Lee's story did more to alter Southern attitudes about race than any other work of art in this century."

The adults who worked on the film adaptation of *To Kill a Mockingbird* struggled to be faithful to Lee's focus on children and their perspective. Gregory Peck (Atticus) recalled that, "To get the kids in that totally unselfconscious frame of mind took very delicate handling." Even so, he was successful. Mary Badham, who played Scout, became so comfortable with Peck that she would seek him out between takes and crawl into his lap. (Badham is shown here with Peck.)

In 2005, only one U.S. senator was African American— Illinois Senator Barak Obama. Elected in 2004, Obama is only the third African-American senator since Reconstruction. However, since the Civil Rights Movement, some general progress has been made. More African Americans have attained positions of wealth and influence in the U.S. in the last few decades.

Race relations today

What is the state of race relations in the United States today—more than four decades after the publication of *To Kill a Mockingbird*? There are many hopeful signs.

One positive move came in 2005, when the U.S. Senate apologized for its historical failure to pass anti-lynching legislation. Had Congress made lynching a federal crime, many lives may have been saved. Federal authorities would have had priority over local police forces, which too often "turned a blind eye" toward lynchings.

Recent "**atonement** trials," which have re-examined crimes from the Jim Crow era, are another positive development. The Southern Poverty Law Center reported that since 1989 U.S. courts have re-examined 23 murders in the South. These investigations have led to 27 arrests and 21 convictions.

Among the crimes re-examined in these trials were the murders of Medgar Evers (1963); Cynthia Wesley, Carole Robertson, and Addie Mae Collins, all fourteen, and eleven-year-old Denise McNair, killed in the Ku Klux Klan bombing of Birmingham's 16th Street Baptist Church (September 15, 1963); and civil rights activists Andrew Goodman, Michael Schwerner, and James Earl Chaney (1964).

In May 2004, the federal government also reopened the investigation into the murder of Emmett Till. The justice department believes that more than twelve people may have been involved in Emmett's murder. At least five suspects are still alive and could yet face criminal prosecution.

Cautious optimism

The atonement cases have given some Americans a new faith in the legal system. Arthur Everett is one of the FBI agents working on the Emmett Till case. Everett is also the first African American to reach FBI management ranks. "For me, personally, Everett said, [the Till investigation] signifies that even though the system of justice sometimes turns very slowly, it still turns."

Persistent inequality

Nevertheless, patterns of racial inequality and injustice persist. Fifty years after the *Brown* decisions, about one third of African-American public school students attended schools where the enrollment was 90 to 100 percent minority. In the Northeast, the number of African Americans who attended such schools was closer to 50 percent.

Another sign of continuing racial segregation is the population of the U.S. prison system. Statistics show an extreme racial imbalance in **incarceration** rates in white and black communities. Racial bias has also been shown to play a significant role in whether or not the death penalty is handed out.

Economic statistics also reveal inequality. Unemployment rates in African-American communities run almost double those in white communities. The economic plight of many African-American communities was laid bare in August 2005, when Hurricane Katrina struck New Orleans. Thousands of impoverished black residents were unable to follow evacuation orders and were stranded in the devastated city. Many in the U.S. also felt that race was a factor in the slow government response to the disaster.

Race and hate crimes have not vanished entirely from the United States. In June 1998, three white supremacists in Jasper, Texas, brutally murdered African American James Byrd Jr. (left) by dragging him behind their truck for 3 miles (4.8 kilometers). Such horrible crimes are no longer condoned by American society, however, and two of the murderers received death sentences. The third was sentenced to life in prison.

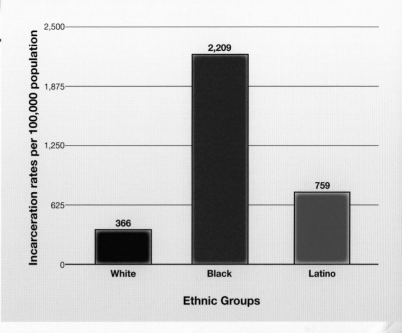

African-American incarceration rates show persistent racial inequality in the twenty-first century.

The concentration of minorities in public schools in the Northeast shows that racial inequality is not confined to the South. During Aunt Alexandra's missionary tea, Mrs. Merriweather exclaims:

> *At least we don't have that sin [hypocrisy] on our shoulders down here. People up there set 'em free, but you don't see 'em settin' at the table with 'em. At least we don't have the deceit to say to [blacks] yes you're as good as we are but stay away from us.*

Harper Lee: literary star

The enormous popularity of *To Kill a Mockingbird* made Lee a literary star. After the novel was published in 1960, Lee received countless invitations to appear in public. Reporters eagerly sought out interviews with the young author. For several years, Lee accepted the invitations and granted the interviews.

In a 1964 interview, writer Roy Newquist asked Lee how she reacted to her novel's success. Lee replied, "Well, I can't say that it was one of surprise. It was one of sheer numbness [. . .] You see, I never expected any sort of success with *Mockingbird* [. . .] I was hoping for a quick and merciful death at the hands of the reviewers, but at the same time I sort of hoped that maybe someone would like it enough to give me encouragement. Public encouragement. I hoped for a little, as I said, but I got rather a whole lot, and in some ways this was just about as frightening as the quick, merciful death I'd expected."

In 2005, Sony pictures released the movie *Capote*. The movie explores the period in which Truman Capote was doing research in Kansas for his book *In Cold Blood*. Catherine Keener plays the role of Harper Lee (above).

Withdrawal from the public eye

Not long after the publication of Lee's interview with Newquist, she stopped granting interviews and began to withdraw from public life. Since 1964, there has been little new information about Lee. During the 1960s, she wrote three short pieces for popular magazines. She also wrote an essay on Alabama history that was published in 1985. She has not published another novel.

Lee's withdrawal from public life has not stopped fans and admirers from seeking her out. But she has remained steady in her distaste for fame. According to a close friend, "Her basic response is—I value my privacy too much to get out in public again on a day-to-day basis. And I've already made my statement in *To Kill a Mockingbird*. She [. . .] wants readers' focus to be on her book, not her life."

Not until relatively recently has any new information emerged about Lee. Interviews conducted in the early 2000s revealed that Lee continues to divide her time between Alabama and New York. She spends about half the year, usually late summer through winter, in Monroeville.

While in New York, Lee lives in the one-bedroom apartment she has owned for years. She is very active, traveling all over the city by bus. She enjoys visits to art museums and dining out. Lee is also passionate about sports. She is said to be a fan of the New York Mets and the "Crimson Tide"—the University of Alabama's college football team.

When Lee visits Monroeville, she stays at her sister Alice's home, not far from the building where she went to high school. Friends say Lee is a great reader, especially of U.S. and British history.

As far as writing goes, Lee will not even discuss that with Alice. Friends say that she continues to peck away at an old typewriter, but nobody knows at what. Alice once told reporters, "When you have hit the pinnacle, how would you feel about writing more?"

But Lee's fans will question that remark. Before withdrawing from public life, Lee told an interviewer that "There are people who write, but I think they're quite different from people who *must* write." Clearly, Lee places herself in the latter category—giving her fans hope to this day that she will yet produce another novel.

Lee attends a Los Angeles Public Library awards dinner held in her honor, May 2005. Despite still closely guarding her privacy, Lee has also faithfully attended an annual awards ceremony held in Tuscaloosa since 2001. It celebrates high-school students who enter an essay contest on the subject of *To Kill a Mockingbird*. She does not make any statement at the ceremony, but graciously meets with the 50 or so winners.

TIMELINE

1926	Born in Monroeville, Alabama, April 28.
1929	Great Depression begins in the United States, October.
1931	Scottsboro case begins in Alabama, March 25.
1933	Franklin Delano Roosevelt becomes 32nd president of the United States, March.
1933	Adolf Hitler becomes Chancellor of Germany, January 1.
1933	Novel opens in the summer; Jem is nearly eleven years old and Scout is about four years younger. Dill spends summer in Maycomb, departing just before school starts. Scout begins school, entering the first grade; Jem is in the fifth grade.
1934	Scout discovers the first of Boo's gifts (chewing gum) in the knothole of an oak tree. Dill returns for summer. Jem, Scout, and Dill sneak onto the Radley property. Scout enters the second grade and Jem enters the sixth grade, September. Macomb gets unusual snowfall and fire destroys Miss Maudie's house, Winter. Uncle Jack arrives and Christmas is spent at Finch's Landing.
1935	Atticus shoots and kills rabid dog, February. Jem chops down Mrs. Dubose's flowers and makes amends by reading to her while she overcomes a morphine addiction, Spring. Trial of Tom Robinson. Scout enters the third grade and Jem enters the seventh grade, September. Bob Ewell attacks Finch children as they return from Halloween pageant and is killed by Arthur "Boo" Radley, October.
1939	World War II begins after Germany invades Poland, September 1.
1944	Graduates from high school.
1945	Transfers to the University of Alabama.
1945	World War II ends after the United States drops two nuclear bombs on Japan, September. Concentration camps across Europe are liberated.
1948	Spends semester at Oxford University in England.
1949	Leaves law school to pursue writing career.
1950	Settles in New York City.
1950	Last of the Scottsboro nine is paroled.
1954	U.S. Supreme Court rules in *Brown v. Board of Education* that segregation is illegal in public schools.
1955	Emmett Till is murdered while visiting relatives in Mississippi, August 28.

1955	Rosa Parks's refusal to give up her bus seat which leads to the Montgomery Bus Boycott, December.
1956	Receives Christmas loan from friends, December.
1957	Submits draft manuscript to J. B. Lippincott.
1957	President Eisenhower sends federal troops to enforce court-ordered desegregation of Little Rock Central High School.
1959	Finishes *To Kill a Mockingbird*.
1959	Makes first of several trips with Truman Capote to Kansas; helps conduct interviews that Capote will use in writing *In Cold Blood*, December.
1960	*To Kill a Mockingbird* is published.
1960	African-American college students organize "sit-ins" in Greensboro, North Carolina, February.
1961	Civil rights activists organize "Freedom Rides" to integrate interstate bus facilities, May.
1961	*To Kill a Mockingbird* wins Pulitzer Prize.
1962	Lee's father, Amasa Coleman, dies. Universal Studios releases film adaptation of *To Kill a Mockingbird*.
1963	Large protests, in which children participate, take place in Birmingham, Alabama, April.
1963	Martin Luther King delivers his "I Have a Dream" speech during the March on Washington, D.C., August 28.
1964	Civil rights protests lead to passage of Civil Rights Act of 1964 and ratification of 24th Amendment.
1964	Interviewed by Roy Newquist shortly before withdrawing from public life.
1965	Civil rights protests lead to passage of Voting Rights Act.
May 2004	Justice Department reopens the investigation into the murder of Emmett Till.
2005	Appears at the Los Angeles Public Library at the behest of the wife of the late Gregory Peck (1916–2003). Peck portrayed Atticus in the film adaptation of *To Kill a Mockingbird* and became a dear friend of Lee's.

FURTHER INFORMATION

The edition of *To Kill a Mockingbird* used in the writing of this book was published by William Heinemann in 2003.

Selected bibliography

Other works by Harper Lee

"Christmas to Me," *McCall's*, December 1961, 63.

"Love—In Other Words," *Vogue*, April 15, 1961, 64–65

"A Word From Harper Lee." *The Screenplay of* To Kill a Mockingbird, by Horton Foote. New York: Harcourt Brace and World, 1964.

"When Children Discover America," *McCall's* August 1965.

Further reading

About Harper Lee and *To Kill a Mockingbird*

Clarke, Gerald. *Capote*. New York: Simon and Schuster, 1988.

Johnson, Claudia Durst. *To Kill a Mockingbird: Threatening Boundaries*. New York, Twayne, 1994.

Johnson, Claudia Durst, ed. *Understanding To Kill a Mockingbird: A Student Casebook to Issues, Sources, and Historic Documents*. Westport, CT: Greenwood Press, 1994.

Newquist, Roy. "Harper Lee," in *Counterpoint*. Chicago: Rand McNally, 1964.

O'Neill, Terry, ed. *Readings on To Kill a Mockingbird*. San Diego: Greenhaven Press, 2000.

Other novels

McCullers, Carson. *The Member of the Wedding*. Boston: Houghton Mifflin, 1946.

Morrison, Toni. *The Bluest Eye*. New York: Plume, 1970.

Twain, Mark. *The Adventures of Huckleberry Finn*. 1884

Movies

To Kill a Mockingbird (1962)
  Directed by Robert Mulligan. Produced by Alan Pakula. Harper Lee was very pleased with the movie adaptation of her novel, which starred Gregory Peck.

Fearful Symmetry (1998)
  Produced and directed by Charles Kiselyak. This informative documentary talks about the 1962 film adaptation of *To Kill a Mockingbird*.

4 Little Girls (1997)
  Produced and directed by Spike Lee. This documentary tells the story of the tragic deaths of four little girls in the 1963 terrorist bombing of Birmingham's 16th Street Baptist Church.

The Untold Story of Emmett Louis Till (2005)
  Produced and directed by Keith Beauchamp. In May 2004, the justice department reopened the investigation into the murder of Emmett Till, based in part on new information discovered by Mr. Beauchamp.

Places to visit

Monroe Country Heritage Museums: Monroeville, Alabama.

Burr Oak Cemetery: Alsip, Illinois. Burr Oak Cemetery was one of the first African-American cemeteries in the Chicago region. The gravesites of Mamie Till-Mobley and her son Emmett Till are located at Burr Oak.

Organizations to contact for more information

National Association for the Advancement of Colored Peoples (NAACP)
  4805 Mt. Hope Drive; Baltimore, MD 21215
  www.naacp.org

Southern Christian Leadership Conference (SCLC)
  P. O. Box 89128; Atlanta, GA 30312
  www.sclcnational.org

Congressional Black Caucus (CBC)
  2236 Rayburn House Office Building; Washington, D.C. 20515-3312
  www.congressionalblackcaucus.net

GLOSSARY

13th Amendment ratified in December 1865, this law abolished slavery

14th Amendment ratified in July 1868, this law granted citizenship to former slaves

15th Amendment ratified in February 1870, this law guaranteed former male slaves the right to vote

24th Amendment ratified in 1964, this law outlawed poll taxes that many southern states used to prevent blacks from voting

acquit declare not guilty

activist someone who gets heavily involved in political activity, often outside the government system

allege claim without proof, or before proving

atonement compensation for wrongdoing or injury

bread lines line of people waiting for free food

boycott withdraw from commercial or social relations with someone as a punishment or protest

catalyst something that starts or speeds up significant change or action

Civil Rights Act of 1964 U.S. law aimed at ending discrimination based on race, color, religion, or national origin

civil rights movement movement beginning in the 1950s, which used nonviolent protest to win racial equality and justice for African Americans

colored offensive name for African Americans

Confederate States of America (CSA) government of the eleven states that withdrew from the Union until its defeat in the U.S. Civil War

consciousness the way people think about the relationship between themselves and their environment

contemporary in the present

cotton gin machine that separates the seeds from cotton

democracy government by the people

dictator someone who rules absolutely and usually oppressively

dictatorship government by a dictator

dismember remove limbs

editor someone who helps author prepare written material for publication

empathy ability to see or feel things from another person's point of view

formative relating to the period in which something or someone takes shape or grows

Fort Sumter site of the first engagement of the Civil War on April 12, 1861

Freedom Rides civil rights protests in which African Americans and whites rode buses together through the South in 1961

Great Depression economic crisis from 1929 to around 1939; triggered financial collapse and massive unemployment throughout the world

hypocrisy pretending to have qualities or beliefs that you do not really have, especially to deceive others

Impurity of Women doctrine some Christians have a negative view of women, believing that the Bible puts men above women, for example, by showing that God created man before woman and that Eve's weakness led to Adam's fall

incarceration being put in prison

integrate end segregation; desegregate

Jim Crow collection of racist laws that denied African Americans their civil rights after the end of Reconstruction in 1877 until the civil rights movement of the 1950s

Knights of the White Camellia southern white racist terrorist group formed in 1867 to fight for white supremacy

Ku Klux Klan (KKK) southern white racist terrorist group formed in 1866 to fight for white supremacy

lynch illegally put to death by mob action

manuscript written work sent to an editor for publication

minstrel often white actors with faces painted black, who perform African-American songs, jokes, and impersonations

missionary someone who spreads faith or carries out humanitarian work, often overseas

Missouri Compromise laws enacted in 1820 to maintain the balance of power between slave states and free states

narrative story

National Guard U.S. military reserves recruited by the states and equipped by the federal government

Nazi Party National Socialist German Worker's Party, which came to power during the 1930s under Adolf Hitler

negro name once used for African Americans, now considered offensive

New Deal President Franklin D. Roosevelt's programs and policies to fight the Great Depression

nigger offensive name for African Americans

Nuremberg Laws racist measures depriving Jews of rights; approved by the Nazis in September 1935

parole conditional release of a prisoner before their sentence expires

plantation large farm that grows crops for sale

psychological mental characteristics or attitudes of a person

Pulitzer Prize any of a series of prizes given for outstanding achievements in literature, journalism, music, and public service

recluse someone who has withdrawn from society

segregation separation of one group of people from another

sermon talk, usually based on the Bible, delivered during a church service

sit-in/sit-down strike strike in which workers refuse to leave the workplace until a settlement is reached

sociology study of human society

stock market market in which shares are bought and sold

strategy plan of action

Supreme Court highest court of the United States, consisting of nine justices

taboo rule or norm strongly forbidding some act or behavior

testimony statement made under oath

tomboy girl who behaves in ways considered to be like a boy

Union political unit, such as the United States, often formed by previously independent units; also used to describe the northern states during the U.S. Civil War

vagrancy state in which a person has no permanent home and moves from place to place without a job

Voting Rights Act (1965) act passed by Congress to ensure the voting rights of African Americans

white supremacy idea that whites are superior to African Americans

INDEX